SWING TRADING

Swing Trading Simplified

A Beginner's Guide to Capturing Market Swings

CHINEDU BROWN

CHINEDU BROWN

Copyright© 2024 Chinedu Brown

All rights reserved

To say thank you for purchasing this book, I offer you a free Video Course and more as a token of appreciation.

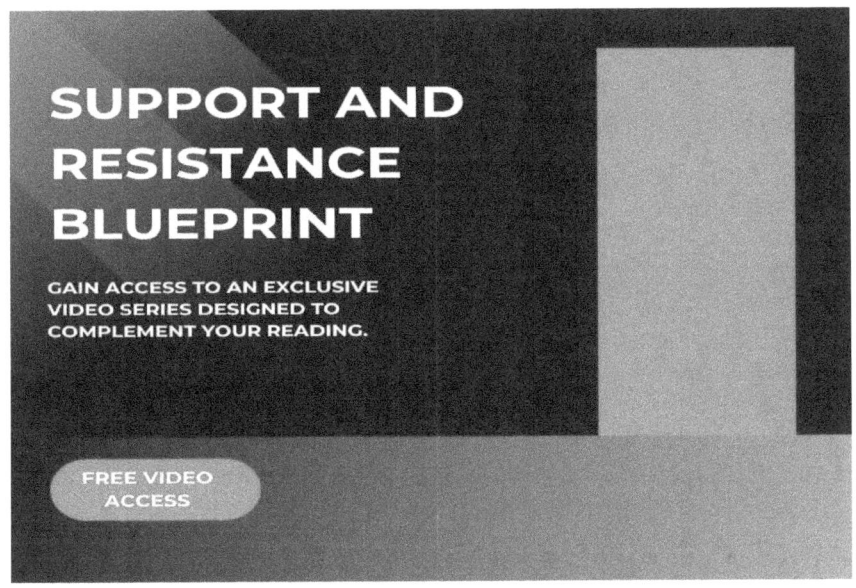

Find the link to the Video Course at the end of this book.

CHINEDU BROWN

Table of Contents

INTRODUCTION	**6**
WHAT IS SWING TRADING?	**8**
THE BENEFITS OF SWING TRADING	9
WHO IS THIS BOOK FOR?	10
HOW TO USE THIS BOOK	11
WHY SWING TRADING MATTERS	13
ONE	**15**
UNDERSTANDING THE FOUNDATIONS	**15**
KEY PRINCIPLES OF SWING TRADING	17
TWO	**22**
IMPORTANT TOOLS FOR SWING TRADING	**22**
THREE	**31**
MARKET STRUCTURE AND TRENDS	**31**
HOW TO IDENTIFY REVERSALS AND CONTINUATIONS.	35
FOUR	**38**
ENTRY AND EXIT STRATEGIES.	**38**
THE ART OF TIMING YOUR TRADE	38
IMPORTANT PATTERNS FOR SWING TRADERS	41
SETTING REALISTIC ENTRY AND EXIT POINTS	44

SWING TRADING

FIVE — 47

RISK MANAGEMENT AND POSITION SIZING. — 47
AVOIDING OVERTRADING — 51

SIX — 55

TECHNICAL ANALYSIS FOR SWING TRADERS — 55
THE ROLE OF MOVING AVERAGES — 55
HOW TO USE MOVING AVERAGES — 57
USING RSI, MACD AND STOCHASTIC OSCILLATORS — 57
CANDLESTICK PATTERNS: WHAT EVERY TRADER SHOULD KNOW — 60

SEVEN — 64

CREATE A SWING TRADING PLAN — 64

EIGHT — 71

CASE STUDIES AND EXAMPLES. — 71
ADAPTING TO MARKET CONDITIONS — 75

NINE — 79

ADAPTING TO DIFFERENT MARKET CONDITIONS. — 79
KEY PRINCIPLES FOR ADJUSTING TO MARKET CONDITIONS — 84

TEN — 86

THE PSYCHOLOGY OF SWING TRADING — 86

ELEVEN — 93

Learning from Mistakes. — 93

TWELVE — 100

Continuous Improvement. — 100
Staying Current on Market Trends — 104

CONCLUSION — 108

Summary of Key Takeaways — 108
Steps to Becoming a Successful Swing Trader — 112

SWING TRADING

To say thank you for purchasing this book, I offer you a free Video Course and more as a token of appreciation.

Find the link to the Video Course at the end of this book.

INTRODUCTION

Swing trading is a fascinating approach to the financial markets that sits comfortably between the fast-paced world of day trading and the patience required for long-term investing. It is a strategy that allows traders to capture the natural ebb and flow of the market, taking advantage of price "swings" over days or weeks. For those looking to combine strategy with flexibility, swing trading offers a compelling gateway into the exciting world of trading.

This book, Swing Trading Simplified: A Beginner's Guide to Capturing Market Swings, is designed to make your journey into swing trading as smooth and rewarding as possible. Whether you're a complete beginner or someone with some experience in trading, this book will serve as a practical guide, equipping you with the knowledge, tools, and strategies you need to thrive.

SWING TRADING

What is Swing Trading?

At its core, swing trading is all about taking advantage of short- to medium-term price movements. Unlike day trading, which requires monitoring the markets minute by minute, or long-term investing, which involves holding positions for years, swing trading strikes a balance. It allows traders to hold positions for several days or even weeks, aiming to capture the bulk of a price swing.

Swing trading thrives on identifying patterns and trends. Whether the market is moving up, down, or sideways, a swing trader focuses on recognizing opportunities within these movements. The ultimate goal is to buy low, sell high, and profit from the market's natural rhythm.

What makes swing trading particularly appealing is its accessibility. You don't need to sit in front of a computer screen all day. Instead, swing trading can fit into a busy lifestyle, making it an excellent choice for people balancing trading with a full-time job or other commitments.

The Benefits of Swing Trading

Why should you consider swing trading? Here are some compelling reasons:

- **Flexibility:** Swing trading doesn't demand constant monitoring of the markets. With a well-thought-out plan and tools, you can trade around your schedule.

- **Potential for Profit:** Markets move in cycles, and swing trading leverages these predictable patterns. By focusing on significant price movements, you increase your chances of making profitable trades.

- **Lower Stress Levels:** Compared to the high-speed decision-making of day trading, swing trading provides the space to think, plan, and execute with confidence.

- **Skill Development:** Swing trading enhances your understanding of market trends, technical analysis, and risk management. These skills are not just valuable in swing trading but also transferable to other trading styles.

Who is This Book For?

This book is tailored for beginners who want to understand the mechanics of swing trading without being overwhelmed by technical jargon. If you're eager to learn the art of trading but feel intimidated by the complexity of financial markets, you're in the right place.

Additionally, if you've dabbled in trading but haven't yet achieved consistent success, this book can help bridge the gap between theory and practice. The principles and strategies shared here will give you a clear roadmap to becoming a more confident and capable swing trader.

How to Use This Book

To make the most of this book, I encourage you to approach it with patience and an open mind. Swing trading is a skill that develops over time. As you read, you'll encounter a blend of foundational knowledge, practical strategies, and actionable insights.

- **Start with the Basics:** If you're new to trading, the first part of this book will lay a solid foundation. You'll learn about the unique characteristics of swing trading, the tools you need, and how to analyze market structures.

- **Build Your Strategy:** In the second part, we'll dive deeper into the strategies that make swing trading effective. From mastering entry and exit points to risk management techniques, you'll learn how to create a strategy tailored to your goals.

- **Put Theory into Practice:** In the third part, you'll find real-world examples and case studies that demonstrate how swing trading works in action. By studying these examples, you'll gain the confidence to implement your strategy in live markets.

- **Develop the Right Mindset:** The fourth part focuses on the psychological aspects of trading. You'll discover how to manage your emotions, overcome setbacks, and cultivate the discipline needed for long-term success.

- **Refer to the Appendices:** At the back of the book, you'll find a glossary of key terms, recommended resources, and a trading journal template to help you track your progress.

Why Swing Trading Matters

In today's fast-changing financial landscape, swing trading stands out as an adaptable and rewarding approach. Markets can be unpredictable, but they often move in patterns. Learning to recognize these patterns and act on them is a skill that can change your financial future.

This book aims to demystify swing trading, breaking it down into manageable steps. You don't need a background in finance or advanced technical knowledge to succeed. All you need is a willingness to learn, practice, and stay committed to the process.

SWING TRADING

As you turn the pages of this book, remember that every expert trader was once a beginner. Success in swing trading doesn't come overnight, but with dedication and the right guidance, it's achievable.

Swing trading is not just about making money—it's about understanding the market and how it moves. It's about developing a skill set that can provide financial independence and freedom. Most importantly, it's about taking control of your financial journey.

In the chapters that follow, we'll explore everything you need to know to start swing trading with confidence. From understanding market trends to building your personalized strategy, this book is your companion on the path to becoming a successful swing trader.

Let's get started on this exciting journey together!

ONE

Understanding the Foundations

Swing trading is one of the most accessible and profitable strategies to trade, but many beginners are unclear where to start. In this chapter, we'll look at what makes swing trading special, what its key concepts are, and why understanding timeframes is critical for success. By the conclusion, you'll have a solid understanding of the fundamental aspects that will guide your swing trading adventure.

What Makes Swing Trading Unique?

Swing trading is frequently described as a compromise between day trading and long-term investing. Swing traders, as opposed to day traders, seek to profit from huge price fluctuations by holding their trades for days or even weeks. This extended holding period makes

SWING TRADING

for a less stressful trading experience because you don't have to monitor the markets continually.

I remember when I initially started trading. I started as a day trader, enticed by the prospect of quick earnings. However, it didn't take long before I realized the fast pace wasn't for me. Sitting in front of my computer for hours, reacting to every market twitch, exhausted me emotionally and psychologically. After a few weeks of mixed outcomes, I decided to try different trading strategies. That's when I found swing trading.

With swing trading, I could spend a few hours analyzing the market, then place my trades and watch them play out over several days. It was a revelation. For the first time, I felt like I'd discovered a trading strategy that suited my personality and lifestyle. This slower, more deliberate approach allowed me to focus on quality rather than quantity, and I began to notice more consistent results.

Key Principles of Swing Trading

To succeed in swing trading, you need to grasp and apply a few key principles:

Patience is key: Swing trading requires you to hold positions for several days or weeks. Swing trading encourages patience, as opposed to day trading, where you enter and exit the market quickly. You must believe in your analysis and give the trade time to develop.

Focus on the Bigger Picture: You're not worried with minute-by-minute price variations as a swing trader. Instead, your focus is on determining the market's broad direction and capturing big price moves inside that trend.

Consistency Over Perfection: Every trader makes mistakes from time to time. Swing trading focusses on obtaining consistent results over time rather than winning every trade. Understanding this will allow you to better control your expectations and stay grounded.

Risk Management is not negotiable: In swing trading, risk management is equally as crucial as selecting profitable trades. If you're not careful, one bad trade might wipe out weeks' worth of gains. We'll go into more detail on risk management in coming chapters, but for now, remember to never risk more than you can afford to lose.

Timelines and Their Importance

Timeframes are the foundation of swing trading. They govern how you analyze the market, place trades, and monitor your positions.

Swing traders usually employ longer timeframes, such as 4-hour, daily, or weekly charts, to find trends and patterns. These lengthier timeframes filter out the noise of intraday price swings, providing a more accurate view of the market's direction.

When I first started swing trading, I struggled with timeframes. I would alternate between the 15-minute and daily charts, attempting to put together what was going on in the market. It was complex, and my trades frequently failed because I was inconsistent in my analysis.

Things didn't start to make sense until I decided to use the daily chart to identify trends and the 4-hour chart to fine-tune my entries. I realized that sticking to a constant set of timeframes provided me with the clarity I needed to make sound judgements.

Why Swing Trading is Suitable for Beginners

Swing trading is ideal for beginners since it provides a balanced approach to trading. You do not need to be glued to your screen all day, nor do you need to maintain employment for years. This makes swing trading a manageable and lucrative approach to get started in trading.

One of my first swing trades included a popular currency pair, the EUR/USD. After looking at the daily chart, I observed an obvious upswing. I waited for the price to retrace to a critical support level before joining the trade. Over the next week, the price progressively rose, and I closed the trade with a small profit. That event taught me the value of patience and analysis, which I continue to apply today.

As a newbie, you might expect a high learning curve. There will be moments of uncertainty and frustration. Swing trading, on the other hand, has a slower tempo that provides you more time to learn, adapt, and analyze.

Setting Realistic Expectations.

Realistic expectations are crucial while swing trading. While it is feasible to make continuous earnings, success does not happen immediately. Swing trading is a talent that involves experience, dedication, and an openness to learning from your failures.

Begin small. Before attempting sophisticated strategies, focus on mastering the basics. Remember, every expert trader started out as a beginner. The trick is to persevere, even when things get rough.

Understanding the fundamentals of swing trading is the first step towards becoming a profitable trader. You'll be well on your way to navigating the markets with confidence if you recognize what makes swing trading special, embrace its key ideas, and use timeframes successfully.

Remember that swing trading is as much about personal development as it is about financial gain as you advance. With patience, tenacity, and the appropriate mindset, swing trading may be a great instrument for attaining your financial goals.

From selecting the correct trading platform to understanding the basics of charting software, we'll go over the tools you need to get started in the next chapter. Let us build on this foundation and continue your path to mastering the art of swing trading.

SWING TRADING

TWO

Important Tools for Swing Trading

When it comes to swing trading, having the correct tools can make a huge difference. Swing trading, while gratifying, is not a viable road to success without the necessary resources. You need the appropriate platform to conduct your trades, dependable charting software to analyze market movements, and an understanding of technical indicators and oscillators to guide your judgements. In this chapter, we'll look at the essential tools you'll need to get started and how to utilize them efficiently.

Selecting the Right Trading Platform

Every swing trader requires a reliable trading platform as their first essential instrument. All of your market interactions will take place on the trading platform. This is where you'll place buy and sell orders, monitor your positions, and manage your trades.

When I initially started trading, I was intimidated by the sheer quantity of accessible platforms. I spent hours studying and testing out several platforms before settling on one that met my demands. However, the process was not without difficulties. I remember switching platforms multiple times because I couldn't find one with the capabilities I required or because the user interface felt too difficult.

When choosing a platform, consider the following crucial features:

Easy to Use: A user-friendly interface is essential, particularly for beginners. You want a platform that allows you to easily place trades, monitor your positions, and manage your portfolio without requiring a significant learning curve. Before committing to any platform, spend some time exploring a demo account. This enables you to test features such as order types, chart settings, and execution speed without risking real money.

Low Fees and Commissions: While swing traders typically maintain positions for a few days or weeks, the fees accumulate over time. Some platforms charge commissions for each trade, while others provide commission-free trading with greater spreads. Look for a platform that has competitive pricing while still satisfying your speed and functionality needs.

Advanced Order Types: As a swing trader, you'll need to be able to place advanced orders including limit orders, stop-loss orders, and take-profit options. These tools are essential for reducing risk and securing revenues without being tied to your device all day.

Security: This is essential and cannot be compromised. Make sure the platform has sufficient encryption and security mechanisms in place to secure your personal and financial information. Look for platforms with a good reputation and feedback from other traders.

Reliability and Speed; A dependable trading platform with less downtime is essential, especially when you need to conduct trades at key times. Choose a platform with strong execution speed and stability to avoid missing opportunities due to delays.

Charting Software Basics

After you've decided on a platform, the next essential tool is charting software. Charting software helps you to visually analyze market data, identifying trends, patterns, and significant price levels. As a swing trader, charts will guide your decision-making.

When I first started, I had no idea how significant charting software was until I discovered a platform with integrated charting tools. I started out with basic charts and moving averages, but as I progressed, I realized how useful elements like trend lines, Fibonacci retracements, and candlestick patterns could be in predicting price moves. It felt like reaching a new level in my trading career.

SWING TRADING

Here's everything you need know about charting software:

Understanding the different types of charts
The most popular sorts of charts you'll see are line charts, bar charts, and candlestick charts. Candlestick charts are especially effective in swing trading. They display the open, close, high, and low prices over a specific time period, allowing you to swiftly assess market sentiment and find patterns.

Customizing Your Charts: Most charting software allow you to customize your charts by adding technical indicators and changing the timeframes. You can alter the colors, add gridlines, and adjust the scale to your liking. Learning how to customize your charts will allow you to build a trading environment that is consistent with your strategy.

Timeframes and Chart Settings: As a swing trader, you'll use greater timeframes, such as 4-hour, daily, or weekly charts. Customizing your chart settings to reflect different timeframes allows you to focus on the big picture while avoiding the noise of short-term swings.

Drawing Tools: Charting platforms usually contain a number of sketching tools, such as trend lines, support and resistance levels, and Fibonacci retracements. These tools allow you to visually identify price levels that are relevant for future trades. The option to draw on your charts is quite useful for mapping out probable entrance and exit positions. Understanding Indicators and Oscillators

One of the most effective parts of swing trading is the use of technical indicators and oscillators. These tools allow you to analyze market conditions, detect patterns, and forecast future price changes. The appropriate indicators can provide you an advantage, but you need to thoroughly grasp them before using them in live trades.

When I first started trading, I relied primarily on a few indicators, but I quickly learnt that overloading my charts with indicators might lead to confusion. It took some time to achieve the proper balance and identify which indicators were most relevant to my swing trading strategy. Eventually, I realized that simplicity typically produces greater results.

Here are some of the most frequently utilized indicators and oscillators in swing trading.

Moving Averages: Moving averages are one of the most fundamental indicators in swing trading. The two most prevalent types are the Simple Moving Average (SMA) and the Exponential Moving Average (EMA). Moving averages smooth out price data over a set period of time, assisting in determining the overall trend direction. The opposite can signal a sell, while a crossover of a shorter-term moving average over a longer-term moving average can signal a potential buy opportunity.

The Relative Strength Index (RSI): The RSI is a momentum oscillator that measures the rate and change of price movements. It spans from 0 to 100 and aids in determining overbought or oversold conditions. When the RSI is above 70, the market is deemed overbought, signaling a pullback. When the RSI falls below 30, the market may be oversold, indicating a possible reversal.

MACD: Moving Average Convergence Divergence: The MACD is another widely used momentum indicator. It depicts the relationship between two moving averages (the 12-day and 26-day EMA). A MACD crossover can confirm the trend's direction, whereas the histogram can reveal prospective momentum shifts.

Stochastic Oscillator: The stochastic oscillator is a momentum indicator that compares a single closing price to a set of prices over a specific time period. It oscillates between 0 and 100, allowing you to spot overbought or oversold positions. Similar to the RSI, a number above 80 indicates overbought conditions, while a reading below 20 indicates oversold conditions.

The correct tools are critical to your success as a swing trader. You will have the advantage you need to make sound decisions in the markets if you have a dependable trading platform, strong charting software, and a solid understanding of technical indicators.

When I first started, I had no idea how vital these tools were. I used to trade without fully understanding the meaning of chart patterns or the indicators I was utilizing. However, as I got more expertise and began to use these tools efficiently, I watched my trades become more profitable and my confidence as a trader grow.

Remember that the tools you employ are only as useful as your understanding of them. Take the time to learn and experiment with each tool. As you progress, you will have a more intuitive understanding of the markets, making you a better swing trader in the long run.

THREE

Market Structure and Trends

Understanding market structures and trends is critical for successful swing trading. As a swing trader, recognizing and analyzing these patterns allows you to make more educated judgements about when to enter and exit trades. In this chapter, we'll look at how to identify uptrends, downtrends, and sideways markets, as well as the significance of support and resistance zones and reversals/continuations.

Identifying Uptrends, Downtrends, and Sideways Markets.

At the heart of swing trading is the ability to identify market trends. The market moves in three main directions: uptrends, downtrends, and sideways (consolidating) markets. As a trader, you need to fully comprehend each of these market structures in order to capitalize on patterns and altered my strategy appropriately, recognizing that patience was essential.

Support and Resistance Zones

Support and resistance are essential concepts in technical analysis and are essential to understanding market trends. These price levels signify places where the market typically reverses or stalls, and they serve as the cornerstone for many swing trading strategies.

Support is a price level at which a downtrend can pause or reverse. This is where buyers jump in to keep the price from falling further. Consider it a floor that prevents the price from sliding further. In a strong uptrend, support levels serve as entry points for swing traders to buy, as the price is expected to rebound from these levels.

In contrast, resistance is a price level at which an uptrend may stall or reverse. This is where sellers pitch in to keep the price from climbing further. In a downtrend, resistance levels serve as targets for swing traders to sell or short, with the expectation that the price would reverse from these levels.

In the beginning of my trading career, I struggled to precisely identify support and resistance zones. I would see a price level that appeared to represent resistance, but the market would continue to move past it. Over time, I realized how important it was to confirm these zones using additional technical indicators like as volume and trend analysis. I began to make better trading selections once I learnt how to interpret support and resistance more efficiently.

How to Identify Reversals and Continuations.

One of the most crucial talents for a swing trader is the ability to predict whether the market will reverse or continue its current trend. Understanding these important ideas can make the difference between a successful trade and a missed opportunity, whether you're starting a new trade or managing an existing one.

SWING TRADING

Reversals: A reversal happens when the market reverses following a trend. For example, a reversal following a strong uptrend could signal the start of a downtrend. Double tops, double bottoms, head and shoulders, and inverse head and shoulders are examples of common reversal patterns. These patterns signal a change in direction and a weakening of the dominant trend. I had a difficult time spotting reversals when I initially started swing trading.

I frequently overlooked small signals, such as a double top or a candlestick pattern indicating a reversal. However, with time and experience, I grew more adept at identifying these patterns, and my entries improved substantially.

Continuation: A continuation is when a market moves in the same direction after a small pullback or consolidation. In these circumstances, the trend remains unchanged, and the price is projected to continue moving in the same direction as before. Continuation patterns include flags, pennants, and triangles. These patterns typically suggest that the market is taking a break before continuing its trend. In the early days of swing trading, I frequently mistook consolidation for a reversal. I would become frightened and abandon a trade early, believing the market was about to reverse. It wasn't until I learnt to recognize continuation patterns like flags and pennants that I was able to extend my trades and capitalize on a trend's full potential.

Understanding market structures and trends is essential for any swing trader. Understanding how to recognize uptrends, downtrends, and sideways markets, as well as critical support and reversal zones, will allow you to make more informed trading decisions and boost your chances of success. The main message from this chapter is the value of patience and practice. Trends and market structures may not always follow obvious, predictable patterns.

However, with time and expertise, you will learn how to read the market more successfully, reducing risk and increasing possible returns.

FOUR

Entry and Exit Strategies.

Swing trading relies on both timing and strategy. The ability to enter a trade at the correct time and exit at the right moment can make the difference between a successful trade and a missed chance. This chapter will go over the skill of timing your trades, the important patterns that every swing trader should watch for, and how to set realistic entry and exit positions. This chapter is all about strengthening your intuition and developing the techniques you'll need to catch the best market moves.

The Art of Timing Your Trade

When I first started swing trading, I was eager to make quick profits, but I didn't realize how important timing is. I often entered trades impulsively, driven by instinct or emotion, leading to a string of losses. It took me a long time to realize that successful swing trading involves waiting for the appropriate moment to act rather than jumping into the market.

Good timing requires patience. When the odds are favorable, you should enter a trade by waiting for confirmation that the market is moving in the desired direction. The best traders I know are not those who act quickly, but those who understand when to wait for the appropriate opportunity.

Here are some suggestions for mastering the timing of your trades:

- **Wait For the Trends to Confirm:** Before entering a trade, make sure the overall trend is in your favor. It's easy to get caught up in short-term price movements, but swing trading is about capitalizing on broader moves. If the trend is upward, wait for a retracement to a support level before entering. If the trend is downward, wait for a rally to resistance before shorting.

- **Do Not Chase the Market:** It's tempting to enter a trade when you witness a price movement that appears to be continuing. But chasing the market can result in bad entry points and greater risk. Instead, search for opportunities to enter with the trend, not against it. Sometimes the best trades are the ones you don't immediately execute. Let the market come to you.

- **Use Indicators for Confirmation:** Technical indicators can help improve timing. For example, if the RSI (Relative Strength Index) crosses above 30 in an uptrend or the MACD (Moving Average Convergence Divergence) verifies a bullish crossover, you can be very sure about your entry.

Important Patterns for Swing Traders

Recognizing major chart patterns is one of the most critical things you'll learn as you progress through swing trading. Patterns are visual representations of market psychology, and understanding them can help you forecast future price moves. Swing traders typically time their entries using the following patterns:

- **Double Tops and Bottoms:** Double tops and bottoms are reversal patterns. A double top is formed after an uptrend when the price reaches a high point twice, followed by a pullback between the two highs. It suggests a decrease of purchasing pressure and the possibility of a reversal. A double bottom emerges after a downtrend when the price reaches a low twice, signaling that selling pressure is weakening and a reversal is possible.

I remember my first successful trade, which had a double bottom pattern. The price reached a low twice and appeared to struggle to fall further. I had little knowledge of the pattern at the time, but something told me it was a good arrangement. I entered the trade, and the price reversed and continued to rise, resulting in one of my first profitable swing trades.

- **Head and Shoulders:** The head and shoulders pattern is one of the most consistent reversal patterns in technical analysis. A head and shoulders pattern is formed when the price reaches three peaks: a larger peak (the head) and two smaller peaks (the shoulders). Once the price falls below the "neckline," the support level that connects the lows of the shoulders, the pattern warns that a trend is likely to reverse.

The inverse head and shoulders pattern, on the other hand, is a bullish reversal pattern that might signal the conclusion of a downtrend.

- **Triangles:** Triangle patterns, whether ascending, descending, or symmetrical, are common continuation patterns. The price narrows between converging trendlines, and the market eventually breaks out in the same direction as the prior trend. If an ascending triangle is preceded by an uptrend, the breakout will most likely be upward. If a downtrend precedes a descending triangle, the breakout is usually downward.

I recall one trade in which I noticed a symmetrical triangle emerging in the midst of a downtrend. I was careful, waiting for a breakout, and when the market fell, I entered the trade. The reward-to-risk ratio was excellent, and I was able to capture a large advance.

- **Flags & Pennants:** Flags and pennants are continuation patterns that appear following a significant price movement. Flags are rectangular consolidations that slope against the current trend, whereas pennants are small, symmetrical triangles that develop following a price increase. Both patterns indicate that the trend will likely continue beyond the consolidation phase.

Setting Realistic Entry and Exit Points

Having a superb entry strategy is vital, but so is choosing reasonable exit targets. Knowing whether to take profits or reduce losses can make or break a trade. This aspect of swing trading is about balancing risk and return.

Set Your Entry Based on Key Levels.

Your entry point should be determined by technical levels, such as support or resistance zones or a break out from a significant chart pattern. I've learnt over time that chasing the "perfect" entry can frequently result in wasted chances. Instead, I focus on entering at a price level that offers a favorable risk-to-reward ratio, even if it is not the lowest or highest price.

Use Stop-Loss Orders: Stop-loss orders are one of the most effective strategies to determine a realistic exit point. A stop-loss is a predetermined price at which you exit a trade if the market swings against you. This helps you limit potential losses and provides piece of mind by ensuring that your risk is contained. For example, if you're entering at a support level, you can put your stop right below it.

I remember the first time I placed a reasonable stop-loss and it saved my trade. It felt like I'd finally learnt how to appropriately manage risk.

Take-Profit Targets: Knowing when to take profits is equally crucial to managing losses. I've often noticed that traders let winning trades go too long, hoping for more profits, only to have the market reverse and wipe out all of their winnings. Setting a sensible take-profit objective

SWING TRADING

based on nearby resistance or price history allows you to lock in profits before the market turns against you. You can also utilize trailing stops to protect your profits when the market moves in your favor.

Success in swing trading depends on good timing and effective strategies. Recognizing important patterns and establishing realistic entry and exit points are essential abilities for making winning trades. However, in addition to the technical aspects, remember that trading requires discipline and patience. You will considerably boost your chances of success in the markets if you wait for the appropriate situations and stick to your strategy consistently.

As you progress through your swing trading experience, practice recognizing these patterns and improving your entry and exit strategies. Over time, you'll have an instinctive understanding of the market, allowing you to successfully manage each trade.

FIVE

Risk Management and Position Sizing.

In the realm of swing trading, it's easy to get caught up in the thrill of prospective profits. However, as any experienced trader will tell you, success is determined not by how much money you can make, but by how well you manage the risk associated with each trade. Even the best strategy can lead to large losses if risk is not properly managed. In this chapter, we will look at the fundamental principles of risk management and position sizing, which are both critical components of successful swing trading.

Understanding Risk to Reward Ratios

When I first started trading, I placed a lot of focus on identifying the best entry positions. I would identify what I thought was a perfect scenario, make the trade, and hope for the best. This strategy, however, quickly led to irritation. One bad trade may wipe out multiple little gains, and I wasn't considering how much I was willing to lose versus the possible benefit.

That's when I learnt about the risk-reward ratio. This simple yet powerful principle transformed my trading strategy.

The risk-to-reward ratio is the amount of risk you are willing to accept in comparison to the potential benefit you hope to receive. For example, if you are willing to risk $100 on a trade and have a profit target of $300, your risk-to-reward ratio is 1:3. This means that for every $1 you risk, you hope to make $3 in profit.

Understanding this ratio is essential because of the following reasons:

It helps you plan your trades: Knowing the risk-to-reward ratio before entering a trade enables you to plan with confidence. You can assess whether a trade is worthwhile depending on your risk tolerance. For example, if a trade's risk-to-reward ratio is 1:1, the potential profit does not outweigh the risk, and it may not be worth entering.

It gives room for consistency: One of the most typical mistakes that beginning traders make is focusing too much on the outcome of specific trades. Instead, focus on your long-term risk-to-reward ratio. If you regularly take trades with a positive risk-to-reward ratio, even if you suffer a few losses along the road, you will be profitable in the long run.

It keeps emotions in check: A clear risk-to-reward ratio might help you remain grounded during difficult times. When the market is moving quickly, it is easy to make rash decisions. However, knowing that you're risking a given amount for a specific possible payoff makes it easier to stick to your strategy and prevent emotional trading decisions.

Calculating Position Sizes for Consistent Profit

SWING TRADING

Still another essential element of risk control is position sizing. Basically, it speaks to the capital you commit to a particular trade. The amount of risk you take per trade has a direct impact on your total trading performance.

When I originally started, I used a set amount of capital per trade, without regard for the size of my stop-loss or the volatility of the asset I was trading. As a result, I frequently took on too much risk in a single trade. Sometimes I'd hit my stop-loss, and the loss was greater than I was comfortable with.

To address this, I learnt how to calculate position sizes based on the amount of capital I was willing to risk. Here's how you can accomplish it:

Determine Your Risk per Trade: Expert Traders risk no more than 1-2% of their whole trading capital on any given trade. For example, if you have a $10,000 account and are ready to risk 1% on each trade, your total risk per trade is $100.

Calculate the Dollar Risk Per Trade: Next, you

need to calculate how much money you stand to lose if the trade reaches your stop-loss. For example, if your entry price is $100 and your stop-loss is $95, the risk per share is $5.

Determine the number of shares to trade.
To get the position size, divide the entire dollar amount you are ready to risk ($100 in this case) by the dollar risk per share ($5). You would purchase 20 shares in this trade ($100 ÷ $5 = 20 shares).

Position sizing enables you to balance risk and maximize possible profit. Adjusting the size of each trade in relation to your stop-loss allows you to better protect your capital and ensure that no single trade wipes out a large portion of your account.

Avoiding Overtrading

Over-trading is one of the most typical pitfalls that inexperienced traders go into. The enthusiasm of the market can easily lead to excessive trades, frequently without sufficient analysis or risk consideration. I've been there before—taking trade after trade just to stay in the game. This typically resulted in poor decisions, higher losses, and unnecessary stress.

Overtrading is when you trade too frequently or take trades that do not satisfy your requirements. While taking a large number of trades may feel satisfying in the short term, it's essential to remember that trading is all about quality, not quantity.

Here are several strategies to prevent overtrading:

Follow Your Strategy: Stick to your swing trading strategy and only engage in trades that satisfy your predetermined criteria. If you find yourself getting into a trade simply because you're bored or feel the need to do something, it's a warning indicator.

Avoid Trading in Choppy Markets: Sometimes the market is not conducive to swing trading. If you find the market moving sideways with little direction, you may want to take a step back and wait for more apparent setups. Not all market conditions are suitable for swing trading, and knowing when to sit out is an important skill.

Take Breaks: It's tempting to believe that you need to continually monitor the market, yet trading can be mentally exhausting. I've come to learn that taking breaks—whether they're an hour or a day away from the screen—can help reset your thoughts and prevent rash choices.

Risk management is just as crucial in swing trading as identifying lucrative trades. You can preserve your capital and make more consistent profits by understanding risk-to-reward ratios, estimating your position sizes, and avoiding overtrading.

When I eventually used these risk management techniques to my own trading strategy, I observed a considerable improvement in my outcomes. I no longer had to worry about losing a huge amount of my account on a single trade, and

I was able to make better judgements with greater confidence.

Remember that risk management is not about avoiding losses; it is about minimizing them and ensuring that no single trade has the potential to derail your progress. The more rigorous you are with risk management, the better your chances of long-term success.

As we get to the following chapter, we'll delve deeper into technical analysis, another essential tool in developing a winning swing trading strategy. Maintain your focus and work on improving your talents.

SIX

Technical Analysis for Swing Traders

Technical analysis is the foundation of swing trading. It is the art and science of analyzing price charts to make sound trading decisions. Unlike fundamental analysis, which investigates corporate performance or macroeconomic issues, technical analysis focusses entirely on price movement and market psychology. Swing traders can discover profitable opportunities while minimizing risk by mastering the proper tools and strategies.

The Role of Moving Averages

When I initially started trading, moving averages were the first indicators I learnt to utilize. At the time, they appeared to be magic lines that could foretell where prices would go. Over time, I realized they were not mystical forecasts but rather tools for traders to better grasp trends and price momentum.

Moving averages are calculated by averaging an asset's closing prices over a certain time period. They smooth out price volatility, making it easier to understand the market's overall direction.

- **Simple Moving Average (SMA):** This is the most basic type of moving average. For example, a 20-day SMA determines the average closing price over the previous 20 days. When the price is above the SMA, it usually signals an uptrend; when it is below, it may signal a downtrend.

- **Exponential Moving Averages (EMA):** The EMA prioritizes recent prices, making it more responsive to current market moves. This is especially beneficial for swing traders, as it can detect trend reversals faster than the SMA.

How To Use Moving Averages

Moving averages are often used to identify dynamic support and resistance levels, as well as to provide buy/sell signals when shorter-term averages intersect longer-term averages. When the 20-day EMA crosses above the 50-day EMA, for example, it typically implies a bullish trend.

When I first started utilizing moving averages, I paired them with other indicators to help validate my trading selections. One noteworthy trade required identifying a "golden cross" (a bullish signal formed when the 50-day SMA crosses over the 200-day SMA) on a currency pair. The trade was a success, which strengthened my belief in this basic yet effective strategy.

Using RSI, MACD and Stochastic Oscillators

SWING TRADING

While oscillators such as the RSI, MACD, and Stochastic Oscillator provide insights into the market's momentum and probable turning points, moving averages aid in the identification of trends.

- **The Relative Strength Index (RSI):** The RSI scales the pace and change of price movements from 0 to 100. Readings above 70 often signal overbought conditions, implying a potential pullback in price. Readings below 30 indicate oversold circumstances and signal a probable rally.

Early in my trading career, I made the error of relying only on the RSI to forecast reversals. I remember placing a long position on a currency pair merely because the RSI was less than 30. The trade failed because I overlooked the general trend, which was very bearish. That experience taught me that the RSI is most useful when combined with other tools.

- **Moving Average Convergence Divergence (MACD):** The MACD is a trend-following momentum indicator that depicts the relationship between two moving averages of a stock's price. It sends buy or sell signals when the MACD line crosses above or below the signal line. Divergences between the MACD and price activity may also indicate a trend reversal.

- **Stochastic Oscillator:** This indicator compares a security's closing price to its price range over a given time period. Like the RSI, it detects overbought or oversold levels. It is, however, more sensitive to price changes, making it perfect for swing traders wanting to capitalize on short-term price movements.

Combining these indicators can give a more complete picture of the market. For example, if the RSI is overbought and the MACD is going to cross below the signal line, it could indicate a potential sell opportunity.

Candlestick Patterns: What Every Trader Should Know

Candlestick patterns are the language of the market. They convey the story of a conflict between buyers and sellers and offer hints about future price trends. When I first discovered candlestick patterns, I was amazed at how much information a single candle could provide.

Doji: A Doji happens when the open and close prices are nearly similar, resulting in a little or nonexistent body. It reflects market indecision and frequently signals a reversal.

Hammer and Inverted Hammer: These patterns point to a potential reversal following a downtrend. A hammer has a short body and a long lower wick, indicating high buying pressure. An inverted hammer, on the other hand, has a long upper wick and can also signal a bullish reversal.

Engulfing Patterns: A bullish engulfing pattern is formed when a small red candle is followed by a larger green candle that totally engulfs it, signaling the beginning of an uptrend. A bearish engulfing pattern is the inverse, indicating a downtrend.

One of my favorite trades was seeing a bullish engulfing pattern on a stock chart at a solid support level. The setup worked nicely with the other indicators, and the trade yielded a significant profit.

Morning Star and Evening Star: The morning star is a bullish reversal pattern that emerges at the bottom of a downtrend, whereas the evening star is its negative counterpart, appearing at the top of an uptrend.

Combining Technical Tools for Success.

Individually, these tools and patterns are powerful, but their true value rests in how they work together. For example:

SWING TRADING

Use moving averages to determine the general trend.
Use the RSI or Stochastic Oscillator to determine momentum and identify overbought or oversold positions. confirm entry and exit points using candlestick patterns.

In one memorable swing trade, I used all of these criteria to purchase a stock that had been in a strong uptrend. The 20-day EMA was higher than the 50-day EMA, the RSI was approaching oversold territory, and a hammer candlestick appeared near a support zone. These synchronized signs gave me the confidence to enter the trade, which proved to be extremely rewarding.

For swing traders, mastering technical analysis is essential. Understanding and using tools such as moving averages, oscillators, and candlestick patterns can help you time the market and spot high-probability trades.

However, remember that no single tool or signal

assures success. The trick is to carefully blend them and adapt to the ever-changing market conditions. These tools will become second nature over time as you develop experience and confidence, driving you to consistent profitability.

As we move on to the following chapter, our focus will shift to creating a swing trading plan, which is an essential step in developing a long-term trading career.

SWING TRADING

SEVEN

Create a Swing Trading Plan

One of the most important steps towards becoming a great swing trader is developing a well-structured trading strategy. Without a clear strategy, trading becomes a chance rather than a planned endeavor. A good trading plan serves as a road map, guiding you through market uncertainty while maintaining discipline, focus, and consistency.

Define Your Trading Goals

The first stage in developing a trading strategy is establishing your objectives. Ask yourself why you are swing trading. Are you hoping to supplement your income, build up your wealth over time, or finally make trading your full-time job? Knowing your purpose will influence how you approach the market.

When I first started trading, my goal was simple: earn enough money to take a long-overdue trip. At the time, I had a demanding day job and limited free time, so the flexibility of swing trading appealed. However, I rapidly learnt that vague objectives were insufficient. I needed to quantify them. Instead of simply saying, "I want to make money," I set a concrete goal of making 10% on my trading capital in six months. This clarity enabled me to stay focused and avoid unnecessary risks.

Goals should be **SMART.**

Specific: Clearly state what you aim to accomplish.
Measurable: Establish a goal so that you can monitor your progress.
Achievable: Be realistic about your experience and resources.
Relevant: Align your goals with your overall financial objectives.
Time-bound: Determine a timeframe for measuring your success.

SWING TRADING

Creating a Trading Routine

Swing trading does not require you to monitor the markets every second, but it does necessitate constancy. Creating a routine allows you to stay organized and avoid emotional decision-making. A common swing trading routine could look like this:

Pre-Market Preparation: Start the day by monitoring market news and economic developments. Look for announcements that may affect your chosen assets. Analyze your watchlist based on your strategy to uncover potential trading opportunities.

Market Analysis: Spend time examining price charts to search for patterns, trends, and indications from your indicators. This stage is critical in deciding whether you'll enter, hold, or exit a position.

Execution: Execute your trade once you've identified a setup that fits your strategy. Make sure you've established stop-loss and take-profit thresholds to limit your risk.

Review and Adjustment: After you've placed your trades, take the time to review their progress. Do they perform as expected? If not, what adjustments should you make?

Establishing a regimen had a transforming impact on me. In my early days of trading, I would randomly check charts throughout the day, making rash decisions. After implementing a defined strategy, I found myself trading less frequently but with higher success.

Writing and Sticking to Your Plan

A solid trading strategy should be written down. This guarantees that it is understandable, specific, and actionable. *Here's a template for creating your own plan:*

Trading Goals

Write down your short- and long-term goals.

Risk Management Rules: Define the amount of capital you are willing to risk on a single trade. Many swing traders adhere to the 1-2% rule, which states that they will not risk more than 2% of their total capital on any trade.

Entry and Exit Criteria: Specify the requirements that must be met before entering or exiting a trade. For example, you may opt to trade only when a stock is heading upward and the RSI indicates oversold circumstances.

Asset Selection: Determine the assets you'll trade, such as stocks, FX pairings, and commodities. Focusing on a few markets at first will allow you to gain expertise.

Daily Routine

Describe your pre-market, market, and post-market operations.

Performance Review Process: Decide how and when to assess your trades. This could entail keeping a journal to track your trades and reviewing them weekly or monthly.

Sticking to Your Plan: One thing is writing a plan; another is carrying it out. Discipline is essential. One of my most difficult hurdles early on was deviating from my strategy. I remember a time when I ignored my stop-loss because I thought the market will "turn around." It didn't, and I ended up losing a lot more than I expected. That loss taught me an important lesson: the market does not care about your thoughts or feelings. Sticking to your strategy is the greatest way to avoid making poor decisions.

Adjusting Your Plan Over Time

No trading strategy is ideal from the start. As you gain experience, you will identify areas for improvement. Perhaps a single signal you've relied on isn't performing as expected, or you're missing out because your criteria are too stringent. Reviewing and revising your plan on a regular basis is essential.

For example, after six months of swing trading, I

SWING TRADING

realized I was overly focused on short-term indications, missing larger trends. My findings improved dramatically once I changed my plan to include analysis of weekly charts in addition to daily charts.

Developing a swing trading strategy is an investment in your success. It provides structure, keeps your emotions under control, and guarantees you approach the market with a defined strategy. Remember that a trading strategy is a living document that evolves as you progress as a trader.

As you move forward, commit to sticking to your plan. While it does not guarantee profits on every trade, it will provide you with the stability and confidence you need to properly handle market swings.

EIGHT

EIGHT

Case Studies and Examples.

Swing trading becomes more tangible and accessible when you witness it in action. In this chapter, we will look at real-life swing trading scenarios that demonstrate the principles and strategies covered in previous chapters. Each example will provide useful information about trade execution, risk management, and lessons learnt from both successes and losses.

Real-life Swing Trades Explained

Case Study 1: Following the Trend on a Stock Swing

Let's start with a simple swing trade on a trending stock. A few months ago, I noticed a potential swing trade in an upward-trending technology stock. The price developed a series of higher highs and higher lows, which is a classic indicator of an uptrend. Furthermore, the 50-day moving average was trending upward, supporting the bullish trend.

Using my analysis tools, I discovered that the stock had pulled back to a good support level near its 50-day moving average. The RSI (Relative Strength Index) indicated that the stock was approaching oversold territory, signaling that buyers might enter. I initiated the trade at $120, with a stop loss of $115 (below the support level) and a take-profit of $135, close to a previous resistance zone.

Over the next two weeks, the stock steadily soared to my goal price of $135. I exited the trade with a 12.5% gain. This trade demonstrated the value of combining technical indicators with a precise entry and exit strategy.

Key takeaways:

- Always confirm trends with several indicators.

- Create realistic targets based on support and resistance zones.

- To properly manage risk, keep your stop-loss and take-profit levels consistent.

Case Study 2: Misinterpreting Market Sentiment in Forex

Not all trades are profitable, and the following example shows how a mistake can result in a loss while simultaneously teaching a useful lesson. Several years back, I was trading the EUR/USD currency pair. The pair had been in a sideways market, bouncing between support at 1.1000 and a firm resistance at 1.1200.

I saw a bullish candlestick pattern building at the support level and felt the pair was going to rally. Without waiting for additional confirmation, I entered a long trade at 1.1020, expecting the price to rise back to 1.1200. I placed my stop-loss at 1.0950 and take-profit at 1.1180.

Unfortunately, shortly after entering the trade, a key economic report was published that favored the US dollar. The EUR/USD pair broke below the support level, triggering my stop loss. I lost approximately 1.5% of my trading account on the trade.

Key takeaways:

- Economic news can cause disruptions in technical setups. Before entering any trades, always consult the economic calendar.

- Wait for confirmation signals before entering a trade, particularly in sideways markets.

- Losses are a part of trading. Instead of concentrating on them, focus on what you can learn from them.

Lessons from Wins and Losses

Understanding Your Strengths and Weaknesses. Winning trades frequently confirm that your strategy is effective, but losing trades are also valuable. They point out areas where you need to improve. For example, my loss in the EUR/USD trade taught me to focus more on fundamental aspects rather than just technical analysis.

Adapting to Market Conditions

No two trades are identical. Markets fluctuate, and so should your strategies. A setup that was successful in a trending market may fail in a turbulent or sideways market. That is why it is critical to be adaptable and alter your strategy as circumstances change.

Analyzing Trade Outcomes.

Reviewing Your Trades: Keeping a trading notebook is a great approach to analyze and learn from your trades. After each trade, record the following information:
- The asset traded and the time frame.

- Your motivations for entering the trade.

- The result (profit or loss).

- What you performed well and how you may improve.

SWING TRADING

Here's an entry from my trading journal for the previously mentioned successful tech stock trade.

- Trade: Long position on TechCo stock.

- Entry Point: $120 (between support and 50-day moving average).

- Exit point is $135 (near resistance).

- The result was a 12.5% profit.

- The combination of RSI and moving averages proved beneficial in timing this trade.

Using Data for Improvement: Over time, your diary entries will reveal patterns in your trading habits. You may realize that certain setups routinely produce higher outcomes, or that you frequently struggle with one type of trade. Use this information to fine-tune your strategy and focus on your strengths.

I remember a critical trade that forever altered my perspective on swing trading. Early in my career, I spotted a good setup in a commodity ETF. The ETF had been on a robust uptrend, but a brief downturn pushed it dangerously close to a critical support level. Excited, I entered the trade without a sufficient stop-loss, believing the price will rebound.

Initially, the trade worked in my favor, and I was up 8% within a week. But instead of taking my profits, I became greedy, believing that the trend would continue endlessly. Then, news of a geopolitical event prompted the commodity market to fall. Within a few days, my tiny gain had transformed into a substantial loss.

That incident educated me about the value of discipline and risk management. From then on, I determined to never trade without a stop-loss and to always stick to my strategy. It was a hard but valuable lesson that has influenced my trading career ever since.

Case studies are more than just samples; they provide opportunity to learn from real-life situations. Analyzing successful trades allows you

SWING TRADING

to reproduce effective strategies. By examining losses, you can prevent repeating the same mistakes. Whether you're a novice or a seasoned trader, the market will always have something to teach.

NINE

Adapting to Different Market Conditions.

Swing trading is not a one-size-fits-all strategy. Market conditions can fluctuate dramatically, and your success as a swing trader is dependent on your ability to adapt. Whether you're trading in a bull market, navigating the obstacles of a bear market, or attempting to make sense of turbulent conditions, understanding the subtleties of each is critical.

Swing Trading in Bull Markets.

Understanding Bull Markets: A bull market is defined by rising prices, high investor confidence, and an overall sense of optimism. As stocks and other assets rise, producing distinct trends and pullbacks, swing traders frequently find numerous chances in these scenarios.

SWING TRADING

Strategies for bull markets

Focus on buying the dips: The underlying trend in a bull market is higher, so it makes sense to hunt for purchasing opportunities during pullbacks. Use support levels and indicators such as the RSI to determine when an asset is temporarily oversold during an uptrend.

Trailing Stop-Loss Orders: In a robust bull market, prices frequently exceed their initial targets. To maximize profits, use a trailing stop-loss that changes as the price rises, locking in winnings while allowing the trade to develop.

During a tech boom a few years back, I saw a major semiconductor stock that was steadily rising. The stock retreated to its 50-day moving average, providing a potential entry point. I entered the trade expecting a bounce. Over the next month, the stock increased by 20%, and I took use of a trailing stop-loss to capture the majority of the gain. This trade showed me the importance of remaining disciplined in a bullish market and allowing winners to run.

Managing Bear Markets as a Swing Trader

Understanding bear markets: Bear markets are characterized by falling prices, pessimism, and a lack of market confidence. Swing trading in these conditions can be difficult because trends tend to be shorter and reversals more frequent.

Strategies for bear markets.

Short Selling Opportunities: In a bear market, consider short selling, which entails benefitting from declining prices. To discover probable entry positions for short trades, look for resistance levels and overbought signs.

Trade Defensive Sectors: Some industries, such as utilities and healthcare, fare better during bear markets. Concentrate on these areas to discover reasonably stable possibilities.

Tighten Risk Management: Bear markets are unpredictable, which makes risk management even more important. To protect your account, use tighter stop losses and smaller position sizes. In 2020, amid a significant market slump, I attempted a swing trade on a popular retail stock. I purchased it following a steep decline, anticipating a swift rebound. However, the stock continued to plummet, triggering my stop-loss. That experience demonstrated the necessity of respecting negative trends and avoiding trades that contradict the overall market direction.

Adjusting to Volatile Markets.

Understanding volatility: Volatile markets have rapid and unpredictable price swings. Economic anxiety, geopolitical developments, or the earnings season for individual companies can all contribute to these situations. Volatility presents both obstacles and possibilities for swing traders.

Strategies for volatile markets.

Increase Your Stop-Losses: In turbulent markets, prices can swing drastically in either direction. Widening your stop-loss can help you avoid being stopped out prematurely, but make sure to modify your position size to manage risk efficiently.

Focus on High-Probability Setups: When volatility is strong, it is best to be cautious about your trades. Look for setups with strong confirmation signs, such as confluence of support and resistance levels and several indicators.

Consider Trading Volatility Products: ETFs that monitor market volatility, such as the VIX, might provide unique opportunities during volatile periods. However, these instruments demand a thorough understanding of their operation.

One of my most profitable trades came during a tumultuous results season. A technology company's stock fell dramatically after missing earnings projections, but it found support at a key level. After the price stabilized, I entered a swing trade and profited by 15% over the next week on the comeback. This trade demonstrated the value of being patient and waiting for stability before entering volatile markets.

Key Principles for Adjusting to Market Conditions

1. **Be Flexible:** Each market situation necessitates a distinct approach. What works in a bull market may fail in a bear market or during periods of high volatility. Continuously assess the environment and adapt your strategies accordingly.

2. **Manage Your Emotions:** Different market situations can elicit various emotions. Bull markets may entice you to be overconfident, and bear markets can create panic. Maintain discipline and stick to your plan, regardless of the circumstances.

3. **Stay Informed:** Market circumstances do not alter in isolation. Economic statistics, geopolitical events, and industrial trends all have an impact. Keep an eye on these variables to stay ahead of the curve.

Adapting to changing market conditions is a talent that distinguishes effective swing traders from others. Bull markets provide opportunities to ride the trend, bear markets instill discipline, and volatile markets test your capacity to remain calm under pressure. Understanding these situations and customizing your strategies to them will prepare you to manage the ever-changing swing trading world.

In the following chapter, we'll go deeper into swing trading psychology, learning how to stay disciplined in the face of market noise and get the confidence needed for long-term success.

SWING TRADING

TEN

The Psychology of Swing Trading

Swing trading success requires mastering oneself in addition to mastering charts, indicators, and strategies. The mental game is often the most difficult aspect of trading. Fear, greed, and impatience may all wreck even the best-planned trades. To succeed as a swing trader, you must cultivate a disciplined mindset capable of enduring market noise, managing emotional urges, and maintaining unshakeable confidence in your strategy.

Maintaining Discipline Amidst Market Noise

The Challenge of Market Distractions: Every swing trader has experienced the sense of second-guessing their trades owing to market talk or a surprising news article. The sheer volume of information available—social media, news outlets, and expert opinions—can be daunting. While remaining informed is essential, having too much information might lead to analysis paralysis or rash conclusions.

Developing Focus: To maintain discipline, impose limits on the amount of information you consume. Concentrate solely on facts and news related to your strategy. Avoid making trades based on others' projections or reacting to every price movement.

Early in my trading career, I read every market update I could find, regularly scrolling news feeds and searching social media for advice. One day, I abandoned a well-researched trade after seeing a nasty review online. Shortly after, the stock recovered, leaving me on the sidelines. That loss of possible profit taught me to trust my analysis and ignore irrelevant noise.

Overcome Fear and Greed

Fear and greed are the twin forces that derailed numerous traders. Fear might prompt you to exit a trade prematurely, missing out on possible earnings, whilst greed tempts you to stay in too long, endangering profits or turning a winner into a loser.

Techniques for Managing Fear

Stick to Your Plan: Having a clear entry and exit strategy decreases the tendency to make rash judgements motivated by fear.

Use Stop Losses: Knowing you have a stop-loss in place gives you peace of mind and ensures you won't experience catastrophic losses.

Review Previous Trades: Consider trades in which fear influenced your selections. Find out what went wrong and figure out how to prevent it going forward.

Techniques for Managing Greed

Set Realistic Profit Targets: Set your exit points before entering a trade and stick to them.

Learn to Walk Away: Once you've met your profit target, resist the impulse to pursue additional gains. Overtrading frequently leads to errors.

Reward Yourself: Celebrate tiny victories to encourage your mind to value consistent profits over pursuing unrealistic returns.

I previously overlooked my profit target because I believed a stock had greater upside potential. It briefly soared, but then rapidly reversed, wiping off the majority of my gains. That incident was a watershed moment for me; it showed me that greed frequently leads to the loss of hard-earned profits. Now, I exit trades with discipline, no matter how tempting it is to cling on for longer.

Building Confidence in Your Strategy

Confidence in your trading strategy does not develop overnight; it is established over time with regular application and outcomes. Doubt and doubt might enter in when trades do not go your way right away, but having faith in your strategy is essential for long-term success.

SWING TRADING

Steps to Build Confidence

Backtesting: Simulate your strategy with historical data to evaluate how it works in different market scenarios. Understanding your strategy's strengths and shortcomings builds trust.

Start small: Use smaller positions when executing a new strategy. Positive results, even on a small scale, can boost confidence.

Track your progress: Keep a trading notebook to record each trade, including your reasons, results, and lessons learnt. Self-assurance can be increased by reviewing your triumphs and areas for development.

My confidence in my swing trading strategy was low in the early days. I would exit trades early or switch strategies after one or two losses. Everything changed when I committed to a single method and measured its effectiveness. Over several months, I noticed constant progress and fewer emotional mistakes. That persistence gave me the confidence to build up and believe in my analysis.

Key Principles of a Strong Swing Trading Mindset

1. **View Losses As Learning Opportunities**: Losses are unavoidable in trading. Treat each defeat as a learning opportunity rather than a source of anxiety. Ask yourself what went wrong and how to avoid making the same mistake again.

2. **Be Patient**: Swing trading necessitates waiting for setups to coincide with your strategy. Patience guarantees that you enter trades at the appropriate time, rather than forcing chances.

3. **Establish A Routine**: Creating a daily or weekly routine allows you to stay organized and focused. Review your trades, analyze the market, and plan for the week ahead using a disciplined method.

4. **Practice Mindfulness**: Trading can be emotionally exhausting, so it's critical to keep a

healthy balance. Meditation, exercise, and journaling can help you stay calm and centered, minimizing emotional decision-making.

Mastering the psychology of swing trading is a constant process. Discipline, emotional control, and confidence are not attributes that you learn overnight; they are talents that are polished through practice and self-reflection. You'll gain the mental resilience needed to negotiate the ups and downs of swing trading by keeping focused, managing fear and greed, and building trust in your strategy.

ELEVEN

Learning from Mistakes.

No matter how experienced you are as a swing trader, mistakes are unavoidable. What distinguishes great traders from the rest is not their ability to avoid mistakes entirely, but rather their desire to learn from them. Every mistake, no matter how tiny or disastrous, teaches you critical lessons that will help you improve your talents and gain a better understanding of the market. In this chapter, we'll look at frequent swing trading hazards, how to recover from losses, and how to turn failures into opportunities for success.

Common Swing Trading Pitfalls

1. **Overtrading:** Overtrading is a common mistake among swing traders. It is frequently caused by impatience, fear of missing out (FOMO), or a desire to recover losses soon. When you trade

excessively, you risk entering low-quality situations that do not fit your strategy.

Avoiding the Trap: Focus on quality rather than quantity to fight overtrading. Stick to your trading strategy and remind yourself that if there are no apparent chances, staying on the sidelines is an acceptable position.

2. **Ignoring Stop Losses:** Failure to set or honor stop-losses might result in severe losses. Traders frequently justify sticking onto a lost position in the belief that the market would eventually reverse in their favor.

The Solution: Prior to entering a trade, always set a stop-loss and follow it. consider it a protection rather than a restriction. Remember that tiny, reasonable losses are part of the game.

3. **Pursuing the Market:** Another common mistake is to enter trades because you believe you are missing out. When you pursue the market, you are more likely to enter late, which diminishes the likelihood of a favorable risk-to-

reward ratio.

How to Stay grounded: Prepare yourself to wait for the appropriate configurations. If you miss an opportunity, analyze what went wrong and move on. The market continuously provides fresh opportunities.

How to Recover After a Loss

Step 1: Pause and reflect.
After a loss, resist the impulse to return to the market right away. Take a step back and examine the issue. Was the loss the result of bad market conditions, an execution fault, or emotional decision-making?

Step 2: Review Your Plan
Determine whether you followed your trading strategy. If you didn't, pinpoint the precise deviations and figure out how to avoid them in the future.

Step 3: Reset your mindset.
Losses might undermine your confidence, but

obsessing on them can lead to revenge trading, a dangerous cycle of attempting to recoup losses by rash trades. Instead, focus on regaining your calm and approaching the following trade with a clear head.

I once neglected my trading strategy during a market rally, believing that the trend would last indefinitely. Instead of sticking to my stop-loss, I added to a losing position, hoping for a comeback. What was the result? A loss that erased weeks of gains. That event showed me the value of sticking to my plan while realizing that the market is always unpredictable.

Transforming Failures into Valuable Lessons

1. **Maintain a Trading Journal:** Documenting your trades is one of the most efficient ways to learn from mistakes. Include information about your analysis, reasoning, execution, and results. Regularly reviewing this information allows you to detect patterns in your behavior and refine your strategy.

2. **Analyze Data:** Look for reoccurring errors. Do you frequently exit trades too early? Are you misjudging market trends? Identifying these patterns enables you to focus on specific areas for growth.

3. **Seek Feedback:** If you're part of a trading community, don't be afraid to share your experiences and seek for help. Other traders can provide significant information and other viewpoints that you may have ignored.

Early in my swing trading career, I frequently felt stuck, making the same mistakes without understanding why. When I started maintaining a detailed trading log, the reasons became evident. I realized I had a tendency to overtrade in volatile markets and misunderstand candlestick patterns. Recognizing these flaws allowed me to change my strategy and noticeably enhance my results.

Building Resilience Through Mistakes

Every successful trader has had a number of

failures in their career. The trick is to see mistakes not as setbacks, but as opportunities for growth. Building resilience entails cultivating the mental fortitude to recover from losses, maintain discipline, and adjust to changing market conditions.

Mindset shifts for resilience.

- **Embrace a long-term mindset:** One loss will not define your trading career, and one gain will not guarantee success.

- Celebrate success by recognizing tiny gains and milestones as indicators of growth.

- Maintain your curiosity: Instead of lamenting your mistakes, view them as puzzles to be solved.

There was a time when I considered giving up trading completely. After a string of losses, my confidence was at an all-time low. But rather than giving up, I opted to focus on learning. I examined each trade, sought guidance, and made little adjustments to my strategy. Within months, my results increased, as did my confidence in myself. That era of difficulty paved the way for my success.

Mistakes are unavoidable in swing trading, but they do not have to mean the end of the journey. By tackling losses with a contemplative perspective, documenting your experiences, and committing to ongoing growth, you may turn setbacks into opportunities. Remember, every successful trader was once a novice who made mistakes; they simply learnt to use those mistakes as a guide to mastery.

SWING TRADING

TWELVE

Continuous Improvement.

Swing trading is a process of growth and learning, rather than a destination. Markets and situations change, and what worked yesterday may not work tomorrow. To flourish in this changing environment, ongoing development is required. In this chapter, we'll look at the tools and techniques that can help you improve your skills over time, like as keeping a trading journal, backtesting your strategies, and staying on top of market trends.

Tracking Your Progress with a Trading Journal

Why a Trading Journal Is Essential
A trading journal functions similarly to a mirror, reflecting your habits, actions, and outcomes. Keeping a careful record of your trades provides essential insights into your skills, shortcomings, and places for progress.

Important elements to include in your journal:

- Trade details include entry and exit points, position size, and timeframe.

- Market conditions include the overall trend, important levels, and volatility at the time of trade.

- **Reasoning:** Explain why you made the trade, including your analysis and expectations.

- **Outcome:** Profit or loss, and whether the trade met your expectations.

- **Reflections:** What worked, what didn't, and what you learnt.

I did not always believe in keeping a trading journal. Early in my career, I believed I could analyze my trades solely from memory. However, after a series of losses, I realized I had no clear understanding of what was wrong. When I first started journaling, patterns appeared. I realized that I frequently overtraded in stormy markets and failed to establish clear exit points. The simple habit of writing down my trades proved to be a game changer.

Backtesting and Optimizing Your Strategy.

Importance of Backtesting

Backtesting is the process of evaluating your trading strategy's efficacy using historical market data. This technique allows you to assess how your strategy would have performed in various market scenarios and identify areas for improvement before risking actual money.

Effective Backtesting: First Steps

- **Define your strategy:** Be clear about your entry, exit, and risk management policies.

- **Select Historical Data:** Choose a timeframe and market circumstances that correspond to your trading strategy.

- **Record Results:** Keep track of indicators like win

rate, risk-to-reward ratio, and drawdowns.

- **Refine and Repeat:** Based on the findings, modify your strategy and retest.

Optimizing Without Overfitting.

When backtesting, resist the urge to over-optimize your strategy to fit past data exactly. Overfitting can lead to a strategy that works well on historical data but fails in live markets. Focus instead on general ideas that are likely to hold true under a variety of circumstances.

When I originally backtested a trend-following strategy, I was ecstatic about its success during a bull market. However, when I applied it to a sideways market, the outcome was devastating. This taught me the value of testing strategies across a variety of contexts. By adding changes, such as including support and resistance levels, I created a more robust method that could withstand a variety of market circumstances.

Staying Current on Market Trends

The Role of Ongoing Education
Swing traders must stay current on economic events, market trends, and technological advancements in trading tools. Knowledge is your advantage, and the more you know, the more prepared you will be to handle the ever changing financial scene.

Resources to Stay Informed

- Financial news platforms include Bloomberg, CNBC, and Forex Factory, which provide real-time updates on market-moving events.

- **Books and Courses:** Continuous learning through trading books, webinars, and courses helps to keep your skills sharp.

- **Communities and Mentorship:** Connecting with other traders in forums, social media groups, or mentorship programs can expose you to new ideas and viewpoints.

Adapting to New Tools and Technology

The trading sector is continually changing, as new tools, algorithms, and platforms emerge. Staying current guarantees that you are not left behind. For example, artificial intelligence and machine learning are rapidly being used in trading systems to analyze data and find patterns.

I remember when mobile trading apps became popular. Initially, I was skeptical, preferring desktop platforms due to their extensive capabilities. However, after using a mobile app during a holiday, I saw how useful and effective it was for tracking trades on the go. Adapting to this technology enabled me to stay connected to the market while maintaining my lifestyle.

The Power of a Growth Mindset.

More than simply technical skills are needed for continuous swing trading progress; a growth mentality is also necessary. Accept obstacles as chances, see mistakes as lessons, and never stop learning.

Setting Realistic Goals: Improvement does not occur overnight. Set tiny, attainable goals that contribute to your overall growth. For example, focus on mastering a single technical indicator or increasing your win rate by a few percentage points.

Tracking Progress over Time: Use your trading journal not only to record individual trades, but also to track overall success. Are you getting more disciplined? Is your equity curve improving consistently? These indicators of development might be just as satisfying as financial benefits.

Celebrating Milestones: Value and acknowledge your achievements regardless of their small nature. For a month did you follow your trading strategy? Steer clear of excessive trading in turbulent markets. These successes strengthen good practices and increase confidence.

For long-term swing trading success, continuous improvement is essential. Tracking your progress, backtesting your strategies, being up to current on market trends, and maintaining a growth mentality will allow you to adapt to the ever-changing world of trading.

Remember that the market rewards those who adapt alongside it. As you continue on this journey of continuous learning and improvement, keep your goals in mind and remain dedicated to becoming the best swing trader you can be.

SWING TRADING

CONCLUSION

Swing trading is more than a trading technique; it is a craft that requires discipline, strategy, and a thorough understanding of market dynamics. As we conclude our journey together, let us reflect on the major points and plan for the exciting path ahead.

Summary of Key Takeaways

This book is meant to guide you through the essentials of swing trading in a disciplined and comprehensive manner, from the first chapter to the last. Let's review the important lessons:

- **Understanding the Foundations:** Swing trading is distinct from other trading techniques in that it focusses on medium-term trends, providing flexibility and opportunity for both novice and expert traders. The value of timeframes, patience, and the capacity to recognize trends cannot be emphasized.

- **Equipping Yourself with Tools:** The correct tools—trading platforms, charting software, and indicators—are the foundation of every effective swing trading strategy. They help you make informed judgements and keep ahead of market trends.

- **Mastering Market Structures and Trends:** Understanding uptrends, downtrends, and sideways markets, as well as the ability to identify support, resistance, and reversals, provides you an advantage in forecasting price action.

- **Building Robust Strategies:** By correctly timing your trades, recognizing significant patterns, and selecting realistic entry and exit points, you can ensure that your trades are in sync with market dynamics while remaining risk-controlled.

- **Implementing Risk Management:** Position size, understanding risk-to-reward ratios, and avoiding overtrading can safeguard your capital and assure long-term profit.

- **Technical Analysis:** Using indicators such as RSI, MACD, and candlestick patterns can help you predict price changes and adapt your strategy.

- **Developing a Trading Plan:** A great trading plan, suited to your aims and lifestyle, serves as your guide through the often-chaotic world of trading.

- **Adapting to Market Conditions:** Being flexible in your approach, whether in bullish, bearish, or tumultuous markets, helps you remain robust in the face of uncertainty.

- **Mastering Psychology:** Emotional control, discipline, and a confident mindset can help you negotiate the highs and lows of trading while staying focused on your goals.

- **Learning from Mistakes:** Mistakes are unavoidable, but they provide tremendous learning opportunities. The ability to analyze and adjust distinguishes successful traders from the rest.

- **Pursuing Continuous Improvement:** The journey doesn't end here. Tracking progress, backtesting strategies, and remaining current on market trends are continuing habits that help you improve your talents.

SWING TRADING

Steps to Becoming a Successful Swing Trader

Swing trading success is judged by consistency over time, not by a single winning trade or even a series of them. Achieving this needs a careful balance of knowledge, discipline, and perseverance.

As a swing trader, I remember one of my early successes. After weeks of consecutive losses, I was irritated and disheartened. Instead of giving up, I took a step back and analysed my trades. My journal highlighted a pattern: I was entering trades without enough confirmation of trends. Armed with this knowledge, I changed my strategy, became more patient, and my outcomes improved considerably. That experience showed me that setbacks may be used as stepping stones if treated correctly.

If this book teaches us anything, it's that swing trading is a skill anyone can acquire with dedication and the right approach. The market may be unpredictable, but your preparation, discipline, and adaptability can make a significant impact.

- **Stay Committed:** Success does not happen immediately. Continue to improve your talents, learn from failures, and celebrate minor triumphs.

- **Accept Challenges:** Every obstacle you confront is an opportunity to develop stronger.

- **Trust the Process:** Concentrate on carrying out your strategy rather than stressing about instant results.

A personal note.

When I first started swing trading, I was often overwhelmed by the amount of information available and the market's complexity.

Sometimes I doubted my own ability to accomplish anything. However, with time, effort, and a willingness to learn, I found my rhythm. If I can accomplish it, you can, too.

Moving Forward.

This book is merely the beginning of your adventure as a swing trader. Apply everything you've learnt here, but don't stop there. Stay curious, keep learning, and strive for perfection.

As you enter the realm of swing trading, remember that the most successful traders are those who learn from their mistakes rather than those who avoid them. Believe in your abilities to evolve and take satisfaction in the progress you make.

Here's to your success and a satisfying path ahead—may your trades be well-timed, your risks minimized, and your rewards plentiful.

Good luck and Happy Trading!

GET INSTANT ACCESS TO THE FREE VIDEO COURSE BY CLICKING OR COPYING AND PASTING THE LINK BELOW TO YOUR BROWSER!!

https://mailchi.mp/8465a286d83d/chinedu-brown-fx

Happy Watching!!

www.ingramcontent.com/pod-product-compliance
Lightning Source LLC
Chambersburg PA
CBHW071100240526
45471CB00016B/2185